What
"N

MW01273868

"This book is a perfect combination of ....
thoughts which create a beautiful anticipation for the next page.
The author made me visualize the early days, like a picture moving
forward. Praise God for people who put their memories on paper,
bringing the past to life"

Judy Drysdale

"This is an expressive and enlightening collection of stories. It gives
us a close up, very personal look at the encounters of a teenager at
war. We get to experience life through his eyes..."

Mitch Huyghebaert

"These true stories have deeply resonated with our family over the
years...we are delighted they are finally being published. This book
would make a great movie!"

The Keith Rempel Family

"Very descriptive, thought invoking.....I cannot imagine sleeping in a
trench for weeks. I feel fortunate to live in the free world."

Gordon William

"We enjoyed your book so much! Your memory recall of your life
experiences is remarkable..."

Alex & Joyce Makarchuk

"A delightful way to spend an evening...was fascinated by the
medical stories and those gigantic syringes the nurses used! *No
Feather Beds* is a wonderful legacy. Well done Bert!"

Shelley & Don Buchan

NO FEATHER BEDS

A NEW TWIST TO AN OLD TALE

My World War II Experiences

And Other Stories

ANTHEA + ROY

*Thanks
for your
support*

[signature]

Albert Gordon Stevens

Royal Canadian Air Force R210354 - AC2
Royal Winnipeg Rifles H-10224 - Rifleman
Lake Superior Regiment H-10224 - Private

No Feather Beds

Printed in Canada

ISBN: 978-1-926718-21-7

"Typhoons at Falaise" by Nicolas Trudgian: I have been unsuccessful in
reaching Mr. Trudgian, to acquire permission to use his picture. I have
used it without ill intent, and will be happy to discuss its use further, upon
his contacting me.

Cover Photo: Albert in Ghent, Belgium - 1945

Assisted by:
Sandra E. Huyghebaert (research, typing, format)
Diane E. Dyck (research, typing, editing)
Managing Editor: Rick Johnson

Published by

Forever Books

WINNIPEG CANADA

www.foreverbooks.ca

DEDICATION

I dedicate this book to my Dear Mother, my Loving Wife of 57 years, and our four Wonderful Children.

My Mother, Ada Mae Stevens-Pearce (1955)

My Wife, Gwen (1963)

Janice, Sandra, Albert, Gwen, Diane, Gordon
My Family (July 1991)

Also, I dedicate this book to the women and men who gave their lives on behalf of us all.

ACKNOWLEDGEMENTS

Thank you to my daughter Janice, son-in-law Keith Rempel, and my grandchildren Colin and Haylee, who have really pushed me for years to put my memoirs into writing. Feeling it would make it easier for me, they even bought me a voice recognition program; when I talk into the microphone, my speech is changed to type. I had been working on it, but since my stroke my voice changed so much that all the work I did was for naught.

Thanks to my daughters Diane and Sandra, who have taken hold in a big way, and now this book has finally become a reality. I'm extremely grateful to them for the time they have spent with me on this book during their busy schedules. My son Gordon inspired me to get going when he asked me if he could use some of my stories at school on November 11.

Special thanks to Gus Henne of Forever Books for his personable assistance.

CONTENTS

FOREWORD

This book of World War II memoirs takes a different road from many other wartime writings. Albert Stevens is always one to see the honest and down-to-earth side of things, and this comes through in his writings. His sense of humor and matter-of-fact attitude turn his memories into very interesting reading.

This is not simply a book of battle and bloodshed, but of a young man who grew up the hard way. Only seventeen when he first stepped up to be a man, Dad had his mother and siblings to support, a country to protect and serve, and a world to defend. Still, he was just a teenager living through many frightful experiences in a very adult world! Although naïve and caring, he was also hardworking and dependable, never hesitating to defend the underdog or protect vulnerable individuals, even in a hostile situation. His story captures the personal life of a young soldier during the war, so very far from home.

As you read this book, think of your own teenaged son, brother, or friend. Imagine that he, in his youth, is living these very real experiences in his own real life! Think of a mother's fear and anxiety.

Things could have been very different for many, had Dad not done what he did. Everyone, especially our children, could learn from this man.

Sandy Huyghebaert

EARLY YEARS

My twin sister Edna and I were born on the farm, one and one-half miles west of the village of Darlingford in southern Manitoba. It was August 25, 1923, five years after the Great War of 1914-1918. Harvest was in full swing, and there was a threshing crew to feed. With my older sister Lois just twenty months old, my mother really must have had her hands full.

Later my eldest daughter asked her grandmother, "However did you manage?"

She stoically responded, "Oh, I hired a girl that year!"

Although we didn't really know what luxury was, with hard work the farm provided most of our needs; it even sustained our family of seven throughout the dustbowl of the 'Dirty Thirties' and the economic hardships of the Great Depression.

As I recall, I was in my pre-teens near the beginning of the drought years, when locusts and grasshoppers came in swarms so thick they would block out the sun. They came in search of anything that was green. We would watch helplessly as they settled upon the grain fields, wastefully devouring only a small portion of the green stalk below the head, dropping the yet unfilled heads to the ground.

The following year the winds came, carrying topsoil from Saskatchewan farms into Manitoba. I can still remember the sight of the three-strand, barbed-wire fences, buried until the top strand was only partially visible through the mounds of dust which had settled there. One morning we awoke to find the summer kitchen door had blown open during the night, and Dad was shoveling the topsoil out the door with a scoop shovel.

A year or so after that, our wheat crops were hit by the rust blight. My dad had to wait for the wind to be in the right direction. Then he would go to the wheat fields with a torch and light them on fire. My twin sister Edna and I watched excitedly as the fields burned, thinking it was great fun. We were too young then to fully understand the gravity of the situation. I now realize how heartbreaking it must have been for Dad and Mother to watch their livelihood burn. There was no crop insurance in those days.

My siblings and I went to school in the two-story, four-room schoolhouse in Darlingford. My best friend at school was Doug Rombough, who lived two doors over from my grandfather's house in town. Doug's father drove a mail route; he also had two teams of horses, which he drove when the roads weren't passable for his motor vehicle. Whenever I visited my grandfather, I spent most of my time hanging out with Doug in their barn or garage. Often we went swimming and hunting ducks or prairie chickens together.

One day after school Doug and I went to the elevator. We climbed into a shed that was caked with weed seeds removed from grain before shipping. The mice had made themselves comfortable in this environment. We amused ourselves by thumping around to scare the mice from their holes. Then we would kill them.

One mouse had mysteriously disappeared on us. When we couldn't scare up any more mice, we left the shed and went back to Doug's father's barn for awhile. Then we went over to the barber shop and visited with the barber. From there we went across town to Jarv Collins' barn to visit his son. It was while we were there that something suddenly bit me on the behind. It was that stupid mouse! It had run up my leg in the shed nearly an hour before and had hidden itself there all this time. I did some fancy dancing and jumping to shake it out of my pant leg, and stomped on it.

Roy Fields came into Darlingford School for his high school years. He became Doug's and my good friend. Roy had had polio when he was quite young, his legs never developing beyond that time. Doug, one of the other boys, or I would have to carry Roy on our backs or pull him in a wagon everywhere he wanted to go. Roy had powerful arms and hands, and was even able to walk short distances on them. He was also the champion arm wrestler amongst us boys.

Doug was a pretty good handyman. He had an idea to help Roy become more independent. Managing to acquire a gasoline engine from an old washing machine, Doug and I mounted it onto the back of a wagon. We attached a pulley to one of the rear wheels for the belt. Roy was able to start the engine by reaching back and turning the flywheel. He would tighten the belt when he wanted to move, or loosen the belt and apply pressure on one of the wheels in order to stop. He steered the wagon with the tongue (handle) back over the front of the wagon. Roy was actually able to maneuver quite well by this means of transportation, up and down the sidewalks in town. After graduating, Roy actually ran his own farm, rigging his equipment so he could operate it with his hands.

The Essex and Students

Dad had the contract to drive the school van for our area west of Darlingford. As early as possible in spring and as late as he could in the fall, he used our second-hand Essex automobile instead of the van. We children were piled in on top of each others' laps, but we didn't mind. We were happy to go by car, even though we had to sit two deep, rather than go in the horse-pulled school van.

When conditions didn't permit driving the car, Dad had to revert to the van. It was a covered wagon, on wheels for the summer and bob-sleds for the winter. There were low wooden benches along each side, and Dad provided the luxury of a foot warmer for all of us to share. This consisted of a metal container with a drawer in one end to hold the brick of burning coke. If their feet became cold, the older boys would sometimes run behind the van for a short while to warm up.

The School Van

One lovely Sunday in the spring of the year, Edna and I were enjoying playing outdoors together. We didn't have toys like kids have today, so we improvised. I got hold of an empty *Flytox* bug spray can, filled it with water, and screwed a length of three-quarter inch hose onto the opening in place of the cap. Swinging it above my head, I was totally oblivious to the dangers of my carefree pass-time, when the can suddenly came loose from the end of the hose. It flew through both the storm window and the inside window of our farmhouse. (See the window between the van and the horses in the picture of the school van.)

At that time my father was sitting in his rocking chair with his back to the window, reading a western magazine. The can hit Dad on the back of the head, and water began running down his neck. As soon as Dad realized exactly what had happened, he got up, looked out the window, and saw me frozen before him in terror.

When I saw Dad on his feet, I figured I was in real trouble. Suddenly Dad disappeared from the window. I quickly came to my senses and ran to the tall Russian poplar tree in the hedge behind the barn. Climbing it in a hurry, I remained there trembling until hours later, when Mother called me down for supper. I never did get punished.

It must have been at the supper table where I heard the rest of the story. Apparently, at the exact moment the can of water flew through the window, hitting my dad on the head, he had just been reading in the story of someone being shot. When he felt the water running down his head and neck, he actually thought for a moment that *he* had been shot, and that he was bleeding. When Dad stood up and saw me frozen in terror, he began to see the funny side of the situation, and THAT, I suppose, is what saved my puddin'!

We had a cattle dog named Towser, a border collie mixed breed. When it came time to get the cows home from the fields, Dad would just tell her: "Go get the cows." She would find them and bring them in, even when they were over half a mile away and nowhere in sight. Then one day she got a taste of a broken egg under the manger in the barn where the hens had free range. After that, no egg on the farm was safe. We depended on the income from those eggs to buy our sugar, salt, coffee, tea, and the like. Mom tried every trick in the book to try and get Towser off those eggs. She even resorted to 'blowing' the eggs, through holes in the ends of the shell, and refilling the shells with a mixture of Sloan's Liniment (the hottest liniment you could get), mustard, and cayenne pepper. Then she put this concoction under the manger for the dog to find.

Later, Mom found Towser in the barnyard with the egg between her front paws. Each time that dog would take a lick of the egg, tears would stream down her face. She kept on licking that egg until the hot mixture was totally finished. She couldn't be deterred, and sadly, we had to put her down.

When I was 16 years of age, I asked my father if I could get a job in town for the summer. Dad told me that no one was hiring those days, but I was more interested in getting the experience than earning the money. So Dad managed to line me up a job with the owner of a store and auto repair shop, who sold all types of farm machinery, radios, gasoline, and much more. He also operated a daily transfer to Winnipeg.

I was able to stay in town with my Aunt Bertie while working from 7 am to 9 pm, Monday to Friday, with shorter hours on the weekend. Each morning I swept the floors, pumped up the gas in the two gasoline bowsers, and filled the oil bottles that were in the racks beside the bowsers. Then I spent most of the remainder of my time washing a huge pile of secondhand parts from numerous old pieces of machinery that had been taken in trade and torn apart. Then I sorted these parts into their respective bins.

I earned the huge sum of $1.25 for the entire five weeks, as well as a one-day trip to Winnipeg with the transfer. While there, the driver bought me lunch at The Hudson's Bay Store cafeteria, which was a real treat for a farm boy. Following this five-week work experience, I had to go home to help with the harvest on the farm.

1

STEPPING UP TO THE TASK

In February 1941, my father passed away after a short illness. So at age seventeen, I had to quit school and run the farm for my mother. That first year the government was paying the farmers $5.00 an acre to summer fallow their land, because they couldn't sell their wheat. We summer fallowed 80 acres, nearly half our tilled land.

The yield that year was average on the land we had in crop. My uncle took over operating the threshing machine, which my father had always done before. Then my cousin and I took over my uncle's former job, driving the team hauling the grain and loading it into the granaries.

Threshing Outfit

Before harvest I had constructed a loader from old parts, which made things a lot easier. It took the best part of a week to build. The dealer I'd worked for the previous summer had an old threshing machine in his back lot. I had eyed it a number of times while driving by, and I knew he was never going to sell it. So I asked him how much he wanted for some of the parts: the elevator, return elevator, and auger. He asked me what I wanted it for. When I told him I planned to build an elevator for unloading the grain into our big granary, he kind of smiled and told me I could have the parts, but I would have to remove them myself.

After I got the parts home and began putting them together, my neighbor happened to come over. He told me he had just what I needed to power my loader. A day or two later he arrived with an old Ford Model-T engine, which supplied more than enough power. This seemed fair, as I had often helped him when he'd needed it. As I recall, that loader later brought me seventy-five dollars at auction.

Some years earlier, my grandfather had set up my father and my uncle with a tractor and some power equipment, but since this was shared, a good part of the farm work still had to be done with horses. I didn't mind working with the tractor, but I detested working with the horses, because the work was so much more tedious. It took forever to accomplish anything. That winter I lost two horses, one of which was really quite old. The younger one slipped on the ice, and although we had it in a sling for a week or two, its condition continued to deteriorate, requiring it to be put down.

In the early spring I had eight pigs all ready for market. I got up early in order to give them a good feed before the transfer truck came to pick them up. When I went out to the pen, I found they were all dead. The vet said it was hog cholera. I had to put them all into a pit, burn them, bury the remains, and then inoculate every animal and bird on the farm.

When it came time to put the crop in the ground, I talked my mother into sowing the eighty acres of summer fallow with flax. The price was much higher than wheat, and the crop was in demand, so could be sold quickly.

We had to buy the seed, as we had never grown flax before. Then I found that I was unable to sow it with my old seeder, so I had to wait for someone to seed it for me, making it late getting in. When it came into full bloom, it turned out to be a beautiful-looking crop, and everyone said, "If it doesn't go twenty-five bushels to the acre, it won't go one!" Well, the latter turned out to be correct; it didn't go one! We had an early frost while it was still in blossom, and I had to hire someone to till it under, as it is almost impossible to plow flax.

When I think back now, I can just imagine how my poor dear mother must have felt. If I'd had a good crop of flax, I had planned on buying a Fordson tractor with all the attachments. Well, those plans were just tilled under with the flax.

2

JOINING THE RCAF

World War II was now well under way. By this time my oldest sister Lois was taking teachers' training in Winnipeg. My twin sister Edna was now living in Fort William with her husband Ken Compton, who was stationed there with the air force. I'd had a belly-full of farming after the crop failure. So I told my mother to rent out the farm and move to town, and I was going to 'join up'. The plan was that my pay in the armed forces would help support the family. We lined up a house for Mom to live in, along with my younger siblings Jack and Doreen; then we had an auction sale and tied up some loose ends.

Royal Canadian Air Force Hat Badge

On December 22, 1942, at 19 years of age, I joined the Royal Canadian Air Force. Immediately, I was granted leave without pay to help my mother get settled in her new home in Darlingford. Shortly afterwards I left by bus for Winnipeg, where I caught a train for Lachine, Quebec, for my basic RCAF training. There we spent endless hours every day pounding the parade square. Basic training consisted mostly of learning the disciplines of marching, following orders, and cleaning our huts! The orderly officer would come into our huts daily to check on cleanliness, sometimes bouncing a quarter on the beds to make sure the sheets were pulled tightly enough.

When I arrived, the camp had a civilian contractor with a large back hoe installing a sewer line from the main gate to the drill hall. It was partly installed when I arrived at the camp. The contractor was given two fellows from 'basic training' each day to help lay the pipes. On the day I was sent to help, we had only laid three lengths of ten foot pipe, when the contractor called it a day. The camp also had a civilian contractor planting a Victory Garden, who worked much the same way. I was detailed to work there for a day, also. Work that could have been completed in about a day just dragged on and on. They must have had 'cost/plus' contracts.

A few times I travelled to Montreal and was surprised to find a lot of clerks couldn't speak English. On one of my visits I went into a bakery to pick up a couple of cookies, and I couldn't make the young clerk understand that I only wanted two cookies. Finally, I laid the smallest bill I had on the counter, and she filled a bag with cookies and took the bill. A few doors down was a shoe shine nook, where I ate two or three of the cookies while my boots were being shined. I left the rest of the cookies with the two fellows shining the shoes and went on my way.

Some evenings I helped the chap in the milkshake bar. I was invited to his home in Lachine a number of times on the weekend, where I met his wife. On Sundays we often went walking along the Lachine Canal, watching the barges and other vessels as they sailed back and forth.

Albert in the RCAF, by the Lachine Canal

Upon completion of my basic training, I was interviewed and asked what I wanted to be. My first choice was to be a pilot; my second choice was for a radio operator. They advised me that the only opening they had at that time was for a tail gunner. I really didn't want to be a tail gunner.

It was suggested that I could take six months general duties and then try again. Questioning what general duties involved, I was told it was working in the kitchen and cleaning huts. So I asked them to transfer me to the army, but was told that they weren't able to do that. Instead, they would give me my discharge; then I would be free to join the army. I was only 19 years of age (not of the conscription age of 21), and also I was a volunteer. I believe that those two reasons played a part in my being allowed a discharge. I accepted and was discharged from the RCAF June 1, 1943.

3

DOING IT ALL AGAIN!

Upon arriving in Winnipeg on June 8, 1943, I went directly to the army recruiting center and joined the Canadian army. I was sent to Fort Osborne Barracks in Winnipeg for a short time, while they waited for a new group to start their basic training at Fort Garry Barracks. During my time at Fort Osborne, I did such duties as working in the kitchen, sweeping, and other general duties.

On one occasion I was guarding an air force person who had been brought in from Portage la Prairie. He'd had an operation, and something must have gone wrong, as he began acting in a very strange and aggressive manner. Therefore, it was required that he be kept under heavy sedation. One night, when I was guarding him, he started coming out from under the sedation. He would sit up and stare at me as an animal might, as if he was ready to spring off his bed at me. It was a long, uneasy night.

Another assignment was at the Fort Osborne Hospital, where I was required to guard a chap from detention, who had contracted gonorrhea while he had been absent without leave (AWOL). As they were treating his condition, he would hold his breath as long as possible, and then he would bellow horrific blood-curdling screams. This certainly made a person do some serious thinking. I think it would have been a good thing if every soldier had seen that. I'll bet he practiced safe sex from then on.

When a new basic-training class was ready to begin at Fort Garry, I was transferred to the Fort Garry Barracks. I got leave to go home on quite a few weekends. One Sunday night, when I caught the bus at the Darlingford corner, I found it to be fully loaded. So I settled into an unoccupied 'jump seat' (a small collapsible seat in the aisle, with no back) about half way down the aisle.

It wasn't long before I fell asleep, with my head against the side of the back rest of the seat beside me. As we pulled into Winnipeg, I woke up to find that I had been sleeping with my head on a young lady's shoulder. She was with her father, but neither seemed to mind.

After basic training was complete, I was transferred to secondary training at Camp Shilo near Brandon. The paratroopers' camp was beside our camp, where they had a tower between one hundred and two hundred feet tall. First the new troopers would be lifted to the top of the tower in a chair. Then they would be suspended there for quite awhile from the overhanging arm and cable outside the tower, before being brought back down. This procedure would be repeated over and over again, until the new troopers became used to the height.

Next they would be repeatedly taken up, while hanging from an open chute clipped into a cage. Once again, they were left to hang there for awhile, and eventually were lowered to the ground. The final step, before they would jump from an aircraft, was to release the chute from the cage, so they would be dropped with the open chute. That would be their first freefall.

One night the paratroopers' sergeant instructor, after one too many drinks at the sergeants' mess, decided to go for a chair ride. He entered the tower, pressed the 'up' button on the control panel, and ran outside to catch the chair, which was already on its way up. He grabbed the bottom of the chair, and tried to mount it, but by the time he realized that he couldn't climb into the chair, he was too high to let go. He had to hang on underneath the chair the whole way up, during the entire time it waited at the top of the tower, and all the way back down again. I'm certain that would have been a sobering experience!

Fox Class at Shilo

Part of our training was an all day 'root march'. At noon each of us was given a steak, potato, onion, and carrot, with which to cook our own meal. I wasn't much of a meat eater, so I traded my steak for another potato, and I ate my vegetables raw.

When we got back to camp, we were ordered to change to our fatigues and report to the obstacle course with our rifles. There were walls to scale, barbed wire to crawl under (while keeping our backsides low), flooded ditches to forge, and bayonet practice with a dummy.

The sergeant was swearing and calling us all sorts of filthy names. One of the fellows just couldn't take any more. As soon as he withdrew his bayonet from the dummy, he swung and pressed it up against the abusive sergeant's belly.

Needless to say, that was the end of training for that day! The fellow soldier was put on charge and marched to the orderly room, but he didn't receive any punishment. However, much to our pleasure, the sergeant was demoted to a corporal!

Toward the end of secondary training, we were advised that we would be going through the obstacle course at night, while they were firing live ammunition with tracer bullets on fixed trajectories above us. It was an effective way of conditioning us for real action. They told us they were allowed 2% casualties, so we'd better keep our butts down while we were crawling over the various obstacles! That sure got the adrenaline up!

4

ROYAL WINNIPEG RIFLES

Royal Winnipeg Rifles Hat Badge

The Royal Winnipeg Rifles (R.W.R.) was formed in 1883, using the Latin motto, "Hosti Acie Nominati" (named by the enemy in battle). During the Northwest Rebellion of 1885, a captured Metis enquired, "The Red Coats we know, but who are those little black devils?" Infantry of the line usually wore red coats, while the Rifle units wore dark green, nearly black coats. During WWII, the R.W.R. was one of the first allied troops on the beaches on D-Day to suppress German troops.

Above is a silver alloy cap badge, which shows a 'little devil' to the center of a maple leaf wreath intersected by scrolls, and a list of battle honors with a King's Crown at the top. It measures about 4.5 cm x 5 cm.

I was given the opportunity to choose the regiment I wanted to be attached to overseas. I chose the Royal Winnipeg Rifles. On subsequent standing orders, I was posted to that regiment as reinforcement, and was asked what duties I wanted to perform. Since I had studied electricity by correspondence as a lad in high school, it seemed natural for me to choose to be an infantry signalman. (In hind-sight, I could also have applied to the Royal Canadian Signal Corps.)

While I was waiting to go for my signal training, a bulletin was posted offering an opportunity to train as a dispatch rider. I applied. The company commander called me in to ask which I wanted, as I was already slated for the signal course. I suggested that maybe I could train for both! To this he replied that they weren't in the business of training people just for the fun of it. It seemed I would have to choose one or the other. So I stayed with my original choice.

When my secondary training was completed, I was granted a week to go home, just before Christmas. I had to be back to Camp Shilo by the evening of December 24, 1943, along with four other soldiers also scheduled to go to Vimy for signal training. I don't know why we had to be back by Christmas Eve, as no one left in camp was expecting us, and the staff of our orderly room was on leave for Christmas and Boxing Day.

On December 27 we were transferred to Vimy Signal Training Camp near Kingston, Ontario. We were taken from Shilo to Brandon, where we caught a train to Winnipeg. There were five in our group, but only seats for four, so we took turns riding on the arm of the seat. Finally, the conductor came along and told us that we could go up and ride in the caboose observation turret the remainder of the way to Winnipeg. There we changed trains to Toronto.

Instead of catching a train to Kingston during the day, we decided to catch one in the evening. During the forenoon, I was able to visit an uncle who lived in Toronto. Then we all went that afternoon to watch 'The Happy Gang' live radio broadcast in a downtown Toronto studio. We followed this with

I'm in the Army now!

something to eat, and finally we caught the train to Kingston, where an army truck picked us up and took us to Camp Vimy.

It was late in the evening of December 29 when we arrived, once again unexpected, as our documents had not as yet arrived. We ended up serving New Year's dinner to the patients with contagious ailments in the camp's sick bay. I suppose the kitchen staff were happy, as they were only required to deliver the food to the door.

While in Camp Vimy, another chap and I were on night guard duty along the southerly edge of the camp bordering the St. Lawrence River. There was a pump house about the middle of our beat, and whenever we passed it, the pump house operator would let us come in and warm up. Sometimes this privilege was extended a little, and we even caught an hour's sleep or so. The operator kept an eye open for the orderly's car lights coming down the hill. If we were inside, he would let us out the back door. When the orderly officer arrived, he would ask the operator if he had seen us. To this he would reply, "Yes, they went by a short time ago."

One sunny day further on toward spring, another chap and I went for a walk on the frozen St. Lawrence River. The ice was covered with crusted snow. About a mile upriver from our camp my foot broke through the crusted snow into water. As I stopped and looked towards the shore, I saw brownish, snow-covered ice, and I realized at that point that this was where the sewage from another camp was being dumped into the river. We quickly retraced our steps and headed back to our camp, thankful that we had recognized the potential danger in time, and hadn't broken through and gone for a dunking.

My signal training was pretty routine, other than one little incident, which didn't have anything to do with the course. One day it was posted in standing orders that everybody was to be wearing the shoulder flashes and hat badge of the Canadian Army Corps. I didn't change my webbing, which was black, or my shoulder flashes and badge of the Winnipeg Rifles. The next morning the sergeant put me on orders, and marched me before the commanding officer. He read the charge in front of the C.O. as "not having obeyed an order".

When the C.O. asked me if I had anything to say for myself, I replied, "Yes sir, it has been posted on standing orders that I am a reinforcement of the Royal Winnipeg Rifles, and until it is posted otherwise, I will continue to wear the black webbing and their flashes and badge."

He said, "Very good. Case dismissed. Sergeant you remain here." I don't know what he said to the sergeant, but I suppose that he told him that he'd better check things out in future.

The basic rate for the armed forces during World War II was $1.00 per day. In order to get dependants' allowance for my mother, younger brother, and sister, it was required that I sign half of my pay over to her. When I went overseas, my pay was increased by 25¢ a day, so I also signed over half of my remaining pay. This left me 37½ cents per day for putting my life on the line! In perspective, this wasn't bad pay for those days.

The biggest part of our signalers' training was learning the Morse code with its dots and dashes, and how to send and receive it. There were various methods of transmitting the code, including radio transmission and light transmission. We were also required to learn how to operate various types of radios, which involved 'netting them in' to different frequencies. As well, we were trained to operate the telephone exchange.

Upon completing our signal training, we all received our embarkation leave except for one of our group. He failed his medical due to poor eyesight and received a furlough instead. Not to be easily deterred, he asked the doctor whether he might be able to go overseas with the rest of us if he could pass the eye test. He was assured he could.

So he went to New York and bought contact lenses, which weren't available in Canada at that time. He was a chubby young fellow, and we all called him "Porky", because he had such tiny eyes. The contact lenses actually made his eyes look quite normal. He passed the eye test, and his furlough was changed to embarkation leave. The reason he wanted to go overseas so badly was that his father was a dentist in the Canadian Medical Corps in London, England, and he wanted to see him. I learned while I was still overseas that he never got to see his father, but was killed in action on D-Day.

5

SAILING OFF TO ENGLAND

While I was in Winnipeg on embarkation leave, I visited my cousin's cousin, Bill Pringle, in Deer Lodge Hospital. He had been wounded at the battle for Dieppe. He shared with me that if I didn't want to get seasick on the ship, I should swipe a salt shaker and lots of bread, because eating dry bread with salt prevents seasickness. (I pretty well lived on dry bread and salt on the way over, as it was just about the only food that was worth eating.)

After my visit with Bill, I boarded the train for Halifax. My Aunt Florence (the wife of mother's only brother Gordon), who lived in Dartmouth across the harbor from Halifax, had learned from Mother that I was on the draft going overseas. She had managed to get permission to take me to her home for a visit of about two hours before the vessel sailed that night. She gave me her mother's address in England.

We left for overseas near the middle of May 1944, on the *SS Ile de France*, a large French passenger ship which the allies took over and refitted as a troop ship. There were over five thousand troops on board, though the ship's troop capacity was near seven thousand.

The upper deck was set apart for officers and female troops only, so it was out of bounds to the rest of us. My hammock was on the port side of D-deck, four decks down from the main deck. Our entire deck from bow to stern was filled with rows of hammocks stacked three deep beneath a low ceiling. We were literally packed into our deck like sardines with all our equipment. This former luxury liner afforded no luxury for us now. Only the washrooms divided the deck in the centre. Fresh water for drinking was turned on only three or four times a day for short periods. Otherwise just salt water was available, which we used to wash and shower.

The *Isle de France* did not travel with a convoy. It was fast enough that it didn't require an escort, and had been fitted with machine guns and cannons for self defense. We didn't run into any bad weather, and the ocean was like glass most of the way over. The voyage was quite uneventful, except for one occasion when a ship was spotted on the horizon. We were all quickly ordered below deck, and the crew was ordered to battle stations. It turned out to be a tramp steamer, and nothing else came of it.

During the crossing, I developed a boil on the back of my neck, and I went to the first aid room regularly to have it dressed. One morning I was sitting on the bench in the waiting room, along with others, as the chap next to me went in to see the doctor. When he came out, he said goodbye, and I asked him where he was going. He replied that he was going to sick bay, as he had the mumps.

We landed in the British Isles at Glasgow, Scotland. As we sailed up the Firth of Clyde to the port, the scenery was beautiful on one side of the ship: the Scottish landscape in early spring. On the other side of the ship it was just limestone cliffs. Consequently we all crowded to the scenic side.

It wasn't long before we had to strain our necks to lift our heads high enough to see the shore. If you looked straight forward, all you could see was water. We almost capsized the ship. The captain ordered some of us to move to the other side, or he was going to order all of us below deck.

When we docked at Glasgow and disembarked, it took us awhile to get our sea legs out from under us. The dock was standing still, but it felt as though it was going up and down, as if huge waves were rolling in. It was the strangest feeling.

6

D-DAY: SAVED BY A LUMP!

The troops boarded a train heading for Aldershot in southern England, from where we would all be dispersed to our various camps. While we were on the train, it hadn't been dark very long before there was an air raid. Of course, we had to make sure that all the blinds were pulled down in the coaches, and the lights were dimmed until the 'all clear' was given.

Signal camp was in Cove, where we signalers were later transported. I had only been at Cove a few days, when one morning I leaned over from my top bunk and announced to the chap below me, "I think I have the mumps."

He said, "You get the h… out of here and get on sick parade!"

The medical officer sent me to the sick bay and told me to occupy the bed in the far end of the building, far away from the other patients. He came by at about ten o'clock that evening to check on the patients, and came back to see me. That's when he advised me that I didn't have the mumps, but as it was too late to go back to my hut that night, I was ordered to move back in the morning.

However, the next morning I had a nice little bump below my jaw, so I didn't move back as ordered. When the medical officer returned, he started to give me heck for not carrying out his orders. When I suggested to him that he'd better take another look, he said, "Oh, you *do* have the mumps!" So he called the ambulance, and I was taken to the hospital in Aldershot.

It wasn't long before my stomach went bad, and I spent most of the rest of my stay there steadily reefing. I would gladly have paid somebody to shoot me. I was never so sick in my life! This was the same time that Mahatma Gandhi was on a fast, and the other patients in my ward said that I was just trying to see if I could fast longer than Gandhi would.

While I was still in hospital, a surgical patient was brought into the ward and screened off at the far end in the mump ward with us. They didn't know what he had, and feared it might be contagious. He had been given a sulfa drug, which was the new wonder drug at that time. They finally realized that he was allergic to it, and he was moved out of the ward. The poor chap could have ended up with the mumps, too.

I was discharged from the hospital on the morning of June 6: D-Day! I guess I can be thankful that I was sick for that time, as the mumps likely saved my life. On Normandy Beaches alone on D-Day, there were 359 Canadian soldiers killed and an additional 715 wounded. I spent D-Day between the hospital and Cove, instead of at Normandy. I thank the Lord every day for the multitude of times that my life has been spared.

7

NORMANDY, HERE I COME

I arrived back at Cove to find the camp almost empty, except for the instructors and about six signalers. We were taken to a hut to practice on the two-way radios. One of the fellows was having trouble 'netting in' his radio, and the instructor went to help him. Netting the radio was setting it up properly to the frequencies we wanted to transmit and receive on. I swung my radio over to the BBC, and heard Winston Churchill sending a message to the free French. He was telling them not to strike yet, but to wait until he gave them the order.

I said, "Hey, the allies have landed in France!"

Everyone asked me how I knew. I said that I had just tuned my radio to BBC, and I told them what I had heard. We all spent the rest of the day listening to the BBC and the messages going to the free French.

That evening the sky was full of airplanes, each pulling two and three gliders behind them, taking the paratroopers to France. Within a couple of days we were moved to just outside Brighton, England, where we were all issued new uniforms that had been impregnated with white powdered insecticide. We were housed in bell tents, waiting to be taken to France. These were large, round tents, which we completely filled at night, with our feet pointing towards the centre pole and our heads near the outside wall of the tent.

At night we stuck our heads out from under the edge of the tent and watched fire shooting from the back of the V-1 self-propelled bombs going overhead. The pulse jet engine sounded like a John Deere tractor: a sort of pop, pop, popping sound. Its flight path and the length of time the engine was to run were both pre-programmed. They were launched by catapult off a ramp near the French coast, and were able to go 350 miles per hour. When the engine stopped, the bomb glided to the target. They were not very accurate. Nevertheless, as long as the engine of the bomb was popping away, we knew we were safe. There were over 6,000 killed and over 17,000 injured by the V-1 in one attack upon London.

V-1 Buzz Bomb

On D-Day plus 9, June 15, 1944, we boarded an LCI, setting sail for France at about sunset. The LCI (landing craft infantry) is a seagoing vessel used to transport infantry right up to the shore. Due to the need to run up onto a suitable beach, WWII landing craft were flat-bottomed, and had ramps which could be lowered at either side of the bow, by which troops disembarked onto the shore. The control center and the engines were normally situated near the rear of the vessel to keep the weight out of the bow.

Along with all our equipment, we were packed below deck like sardines, barely leaving us enough room to move around. It was so hot and stuffy below deck that I couldn't sleep, so I went up to the main deck and noticed an open doorway while walking about. Looking in, I found it was the engine room, and down the stairs I went. The ship was powered by four big twelve cylinder diesel engines, two on each side in tandem, driving the two huge propellers. The noise was so great that it was virtually impossible for the engineer and me to hear each other talk, so we spent the rest of the night writing messages back and forth.

Near morning the engineer advised me that I'd better return to my deck, as we were approaching France, and I would have to put my gear on and be ready to disembark. When we approached the shore, the nose of the LCI was eased up onto the Normandy beach, the gang planks were lowered on either side of the bow, and we disembarked.

LCI (Landing Craft Infantry)

8

ASHORE IN FRANCE

We spent the rest of the day marching inland from the beach. We hadn't gone far before we came upon some English troops having their morning 'spot of tea'. By evening we came to a cow pasture, where we were told to 'dig in'. Another chap and I, not ever having dug a slit trench before, decided to dig one wide enough for the two of us. With our comfort in mind, we dug it deep enough so we could easily sit up in it, moving a lot more dirt than necessary. We found some old wood and covered most of the trench over. I never bothered to go to that kind of trouble again.

Later, after bedding down for the night, we heard a little noise inside the trench. As my partner struck a match to see what it was, it soon became apparent that we had dug down beneath the tunnels of some huge beetles about the shape and size of half a walnut, with legs the size of match sticks. Earlier, we had removed our jackets, shoes, and gators, but I can tell you, we weren't long putting them back on and doing them up as tightly as possible. We weren't sure whether these things were going to have a feed on us, or what might happen, but they actually didn't bother us at all. They were only trying to make their way across us and up the other side of the trench into their tunnels.

We spent the next day, June 16 or so, working our way closer to the front near Caen, where we arrived at a holding unit. We did whatever they needed us to do while waiting until one of our regiments required a replacement signaler.

One of the duties assigned me was on a burial party, digging temporary graves for around fifty RWR personnel killed in the battle for the Carpiquet Airport on July 4 and 5. That battle had required a second assault, as the first assault had failed. That evening I didn't enjoy my food!

Toward July 16 another chap and I were put on guard duty at an artillery ammunitions storage site very close to Caen. At night, we took turns sleeping and guarding the ammunitions dump. One morning I woke up to a horrible roar, and the ground was shaking beneath me. I was fearful of raising my head above the slit trench, until my partner, who had been taking his turn on guard, came and advised me that the battle for Caen had begun.

The incessant roar was the sound of wave after wave of airplanes, and bombs exploding. Our field artillery right in front of us was continuously shelling Caen, and the heavy anti-aircraft guns behind us were continually firing over our heads. The ammunition site we were guarding was about the size of a football field, and one stray shell would have set off a spectacular 'Fourth of July' fireworks display! Later, when Caen was secured, we moved through the outskirts of the city, which appeared as though a huge tornado had flattened it.

9

I'M WITH MY REGIMENT

After Caen I was called up from the holding unit to front line action as a signaler with my regiment, the Royal Winnipeg Rifles. We headed toward the Falaise Gap. We were told to dig in about half a mile from The Gap, where we remained until it was secured. My partner and I had dug a slit trench large enough for the telephone exchange at one end, with enough room for one of us to sleep behind the exchange operator. Towards morning, while I was sleeping and my partner was operating the exchange, a shell hit about 25 or 30 feet away, caving in our trench. I was nearly covered with dirt, and my partner had to help me dig out.

Later we learned that a dispatch rider had arrived prior to this with a message for the Commanding Officer. He had been told there was an empty slit trench nearby that he could use to get some sleep, and that the cook was just starting breakfast, if he wanted anything to eat or drink. The dispatcher had put his bike and bag by the slit trench, and went off to see the cook. Shortly afterwards, the same shell that caved in our slit trench made a direct hit on his bike. All that was left of that bike was one wheel. The rest was blown to pieces. Had he been in his trench, he definitely would have been killed.

Sometime later my partner and I were out laying a telephone line to one of our companies, when the sergeant major came along in his jeep. He was talking to my partner, and I was standing near the back of the jeep, when we suddenly came under heavy shell fire. The sergeant major hollered, "Jump in!"

My partner managed to jump in, but I was only able to grab the spare tire on the back as he took off at full speed. My feet were flying out behind me as we bounced over the field.

Some Royal Winnipeg Rifle Signalers
(I'm in the middle.)

At Falaise Gap the allied forces had the enemy on the run and endeavoring to retreat across the Seine River. The ground battle was assisted by Typhoon fighter/bomber planes firing rockets at the German tanks and other equipment. From our position we were able to watch these planes as they swooped down to strike the enemy equipment time after time. The planes knocked out much of the enemy equipment, causing most of the German soldiers in that area, who were not killed, to surrender. This was a major turning point for the allies. We destroyed most of the German forces and equipment west of the Seine River. Hundreds of German prisoners marched past us three or more abreast with their hands on their heads, as they were taken back to a P.O.W. camp.

Typhoons at Falaise — Nicolas Trudgian

The Battle at Falaise Gap was August 7 to 22, 1944.

Now we were able to move forward much faster for awhile. At one point I was in a Bren gun carrier (a small tracked vehicle) operating the radio. Suddenly, we came under shell fire on the road just ahead of us. The driver took off across the field at top speed, to get out of range and to get around the area that was being shelled. That was a pretty close call.

We had been moving up all day, and when we stopped for the night, I showed the sergeant major the blister that had broken on my hand and the red streak going up my arm. Obviously blood poisoning was setting in. He was very unhappy with me and gave me heck for not having told him in the morning, when we were closer to the field hospital. I told him that it was just a blister in the morning and wasn't bothering me then. I guess there was so much dirt that it didn't take long for infection to set in. He had to take me back in his jeep to a first aid unit, where I was transferred to an ambulance. We spent the night heading back toward a field hospital.

Towards morning the ambulance came upon a spot where a bomb had blown a huge crater in the road. It hadn't been there earlier in the day. We had to drive across the ditch, into a field, and back up onto the road to get around the crater.

In the morning the driver stopped at a building and went in. At about the same time, a bomb exploded on the opposite side of the building. Slate shingles from the roof rained down like hail on the ambulance. The driver returned and informed us that the bomb, which had just exploded, had actually landed in the courtyard sometime during the night.

We headed back to the field hospital, which was established in a number of tents. There they operated on my hand. I 'came to' on a stretcher on the ground in another tent, and an orderly was there with me. They had given me sodium pentothal for the operation, and I was spilling my guts. I couldn't stop talking, no matter how hard I tried. I found myself telling them everything about my life, and was feeling so stupid. I imagine they had many laughs whenever they used sodium pentothal, otherwise known as 'truth serum'.

After this I was sent a little further back to an army hospital, which was also established in tents. I was taking a shot of penicillin everyday in the butt, and I can't remember why I was a bed patient. It must have been shortly after my surgery. The 'up patients' were lined up to get the meal trays for the 'bed patients' before they got their own.

At some point the nurse came around to give us our shots of penicillin for the day. I hadn't seen the size of the needle, until the chap at the foot of my bed in the lineup was told to drop his drawers. The nurse had this syringe about half an inch in diameter and about four or five inches long, loaded with penicillin, with a needle on the end like a two inch nail. She attempted to drive it into the side of his butt, but had to pull back and take a second drive.

It turned out that I was next in line for mine, and boy, did it hurt after seeing what I was in for! They didn't change needles in those days. They just wiped them off with alcohol and gave the required amount to the next patient until the syringe was empty, refilled it, and carried on. It was a far cry from how they have to do things in this day and age. I guess they thought it was the miracle drug and nothing could live in it.

The chap in the bed next to me had worked for the railroad. The army had taken over some of the French trains to move supplies, and now he was with that particular unit. One day a friend of his from the unit came to visit him, and he introduced him to me.

When I was discharged from the army and living in Flin Flon after the war, I was having a coffee with George Lewis at the counter in the Northern Café. I heard somebody talking down near the other end of the counter, and I said to George, "I know that voice! That's Miles Anderson. His friend in the hospital in France introduced me to him." I had never seen or talked to him since, but he has the type of voice that you'll never forget, very deep, and he speaks rather slowly.

George said, "That's right, that's Miles Anderson", and George reintroduced me to Miles. I reminded him of the occasion where he had been introduced to me in France, and he was surprised that I remembered him. So was I, although he had the type of voice that you could easily pick out in a crowd.

I spent about a week or more at the hospital before returning to the Royal Winnipeg Rifles. During a bit of a break, we were marched to the English Channel where, under orders, we peeled off our clothes on the beach and went in for a swim. There were dozens of French women in swimming as we waded into the channel. We only had time for a short swim, when we were ordered to get dressed again and were marched back to camp. I guess it was a way of giving us a bath, albeit in salty water, and without a change of clothes or towels. Obviously the luxury of hot showers wasn't readily available to us.

Some weeks later we were marched over to another location, where there were three large tents set up. We peeled off all our clothes in the first tent, and continued through to the second tent, which housed a mobile shower. After having a good shower, we proceeded to the third tent, where we were issued all new clothes. Other than these two occasions, I don't ever remember having another shower or bath in the field.

10

DODGING THE BULLETS

One evening after moving up closer to the front, we stopped at a gated area, and I was given the task of laying a telephone line from headquarters to one of the company locations. I had just managed to lay it from the exchange through the front gate, and was laying it along the base of the outside wall, when I heard a bunch of troops marching up the road toward me. I was afraid they were German troops.

When they got abreast of where I was, I heard their commander holler, "Achtung, halt" (achtung being the German word for attention).

I thought, "Oh, they've seen me!" I wasn't sure what was going to happen when the leader started walking toward me. It turned out that it was only a chap from the Polish army, which must have been nearby, with a bunch of German prisoners. He asked me where the prisoner compound was, so I directed him to go inside the gated area, where he could get directions from our commanding officer.

Another time we moved into a valley, where we dug in. I was operating the telephone exchange that night, and the sergeant major came over to tell one of the officers and myself that we were to advise all personnel to keep as still as possible, and to take steps for complete concealment. I was by myself all night. In the morning the sergeant major was pretty upset when he saw some movement at one of the company locations about a half mile away. He came to me and asked if I had scnt the message for them to keep still and out of sight. We were on radio silence, and I didn't have a phone line in as yet. I told him that the runner hadn't come, so I couldn't send the message to that company. I was then given the task of laying the phone line.

I took off with a number of reels of wire and headed in the direction of the other company. It wasn't too long before a sniper across the valley started shooting at me, kicking up the dust around my feet. Every time I came to the end of a reel of cable, I would put the reels in front of me, staying in line with them to make as small a target as possible. When I got the new reel of cable attached, I would get up and take off on the run again. Finally I reached the company and connected their phone, but in testing it, I couldn't get through to headquarters.

While still under occasional sniper fire, I had to trace my line back to see where it was broken. I found that a Dragoon company had moved in, gone over my line with their vehicles, and cut off the line. Connecting another reel to the line, I had to reroute it behind a row of trees to avoid this location. Finding myself in a dry creek bed with trees growing over it like an archway, I began laying the telephone line up the creek bed. The cradle that the reel fits on had a ratchet on it to keep from spinning off an extra length of line when you stopped moving. It went 'clickety-click' as it turned.

All of a sudden I heard someone shout, "Halt!" I looked up to see a couple of rifles pointed at me.

The officer said to me, "You just scared the h… out of us!" They informed me that the Germans had just started using a small radio-controlled robot tank loaded with explosives. The sound of the ratchet was like the sound that the tracks on the robot tank would have made. It could have done a lot of damage to our equipment.

They then suggested to me, "When you are laying the line like that, you should either sing or whistle. We just about blasted you off the face of the Earth!!"

Telling them about the sniper, I pointed out the location where I had noticed the flashes of gunfire. They moved a vehicle up through the trees and fired a couple of rounds in that direction. I continued laying my line, and managed to connect it to the end of the line coming from the company. Re-checking the phone and finding I had finally been successful, I headed back to headquarters with no more interference from the sniper.

Arriving back at headquarters, I found the sergeant major was quite mad at me for having taken so long. He told me they were just about ready to send out a search party to find me. He didn't wait for any explanation from me, so he never understood the difficulties I had faced. Then he put me under open arrest. Thanks a lot!

I was given a lot of jobs to do absolutely on my own, without a partner. I guess that's because I never refused to do what I was told, and was always willing to go alone, without asking for help.

One night we moved up about four or five times. Every time we stopped, we were ordered to dig in. There was a lot of limestone, and we had to do quite a bit of picking to dig our trench. The last time we were told to dig in, I was so tired that I just lay down under a tree and went to sleep.

I guess I must have told some of the guys that my biggest fear whenever I dug in was, if we should be overtaken by the Germans, I might sleep in and be taken prisoner. Later that night they took some German prisoners. Knowing of my fear, and partly because I had been too lazy to dig in, they sat the prisoners down in a circle all around me.

When I woke up in the morning I could hear foreign voices, and the first thing that came to mind was, "Oh my God, it has happened!" Afraid for awhile even to open my eyes, I was just lying there with sweat pouring off my face! Finally I squinted a little bit and could see our fellows standing behind these prisoners with big smiles on their faces, waiting for my reaction when I 'came to'. They thought it was a great big joke!

Once after moving up all day, we turned into a field beside the road, and our cook started setting up the system to prepare our dinner. An American group happened to be camped across the road from us. Their commanding officer came over and asked our commander if the boys had eaten dinner yet. Our C.O. informed him that the cook was just setting up. He said, "Bring the boys across; we have lots of food over there."

We were all marched across the road to a huge tent. Upon entering the tent, we saw a long table with benches on both sides, all set up with porcelain plates, cups, and cutlery. We were treated to a full fowl dinner with all the trimmings.

I thought, "Boy, we are sure in the wrong army!" Their cooks had stainless steel propane stoves with ovens, and they had German prisoners doing the cooking, serving, and cleaning up. It was certainly different from what we were used to.

Nesting Mess Tins

On the other hand, our cooking was done with big vats on rows of cement blocks with buffalo torches at each end. We

had a pair of mess tins about four inches wide, six inches long, and two inches deep, with a folding wire handle at one end. One tin was slightly smaller and fit inside the larger one face to face. They were carried in straps on our webbing. These were used for eating and drinking, shaving, and washing ourselves. They were used for everything!

Our regular food, as I can recall, was British rations, which mostly consisted of canned Argentine mutton stew, and steak and kidney pie, served alternately day after day. I can recall getting our Canadian rations, which were much more desirable, only twice while in the field.

A lot of people may not realize that up until sometime after the war, the only Canadian citizens were the Canadian Natives. It was not until January 1, 1947, when the Canadian Citizenship Act was signed, that we could legally call ourselves Canadians. Up until that time, we bore the racial origin of our father. Therefore, when we arrived overseas, being that we were part of the British Commonwealth, we were attached to the British armed forces and drew our rations from the British Service Corps.

One day we were preparing to start an attack under a creeping barrage of our own artillery fire. We were about ready to leave our location and start the attack, when the artillery began laying down the creeping barrage. They either got their coordinates mixed up or their range wrong, because they laid the barrage down right around us. We all dove to get into buildings.

I tried to contact headquarters on the radio to advise them that the barrage was laid down short of its required location, but I couldn't get through to them. With shells exploding all around, I had to go back out to the courtyard, where I finally managed to contact headquarters and give them the information. They had the creeping barrage stopped, and called off the attack.

I can say that any artillery fire from the Germans couldn't hold a candle to the barrage from our own artillery.

11

SLEEPING IN A GRAVE

Once again we'd been moving forward most of the day, and we stopped for the night in an orchard. The apples in the area where our company was must have been mostly for cider, because they were as bitter as the devil, except for one tree. It had lovely eating apples. When we were told to dig in for the night, another chap and I dug in near this tree. I don't know if this was the reason that these apples were so good, but we each dug out a skeleton. Of course, when you have to pick most of the way because of the limestone, you aren't about to look for another location. We could both say that we have slept in a grave.

One time we came upon a large cave and were told that we would spend the night there. I thought it was great to get in some place where I could remove my boots for a change. I had placed them beside me while I slept. The soldier who was supposed to be guarding certainly didn't do a very good job, as apparently a Frenchman had come and stolen my boots that night. I had to wear my fatigue shoes (canvas-topped oxfords) for a day or two, until they managed to get a pair of British army boots for me. The dye in those boots wasn't fast like our own. After getting wet a few times, my feet were a solid black up to the top of the boots.

There was another time when we moved back from the front for a bit of a rest. Our regiment was camped in a field just a short distance from a small town in France, so some of our troops went into town quite regularly.

One day I noticed a lot of civilians lined up on both sides of the road between the town and our camp. I went to see what it was all about. There was a Canadian soldier, not from our regiment, who I believe must have been somewhat intoxicated, with a skinned lamb's head under his arm. He was walking along chewing the lamb's tongue. I imagine he was not yet tired of mutton!

When we were about to enter Calais on the coast of France, we were advised that the people of Calais had been given a chance to vacate the city before the attack would begin. It was around September 28 when the bombers started bombing Calais. German anti-aircraft guns were firing at the planes. A badly disabled flying fortress crashed in a field and burned not far from where we were waiting to enter the city.

As soon as the planes all left, we entered the city with very little resistance and took a considerable number of prisoners. I overheard one of the men suggest that we should just take them behind the building and shoot them. I made it very clear to him that he had better not, or I would turn him in to the commanding officer. If we were ever taken prisoner, how could we expect to be treated any differently? Sadly, the things that troops go through during war can muster attitudes of this sort.

We spent a couple of days in Calais before proceeding on to Belgium, where we had a few days' break.

12

BELGIUM: THE LEOPOLD CANAL

We were gathered close to the Leopold Canal in Belgium, waiting for the engineers to get a suspension foot bridge across the canal. It was about ten o'clock in the evening, somewhere around October 6, when my company commander asked me to go back to headquarters and coordinate my watch with headquarters' time, so we would all move out simultaneously. On my way there it was dark enough that all I could see were the silhouettes of trees and buildings. I knew I was on the road by the sound of my boots on the cobblestone.

All of a sudden, the area lit up like daylight and there was one huge boom! I went about six feet in the air and never stopped running until I reached headquarters. There they advised me that it had been our own artillery, and that they possibly thought I was a German and fired one of their cannons at me. It must have missed me, as I'm still here! I'm sure they would have had a good laugh when they saw that it was one of their own soldiers, but it wasn't funny to me. After coordinating the time, I returned to my own company.

Close to midnight we moved out and headed for the now completed suspension foot bridge over the Leopold Canal. We were within about one-eighth of a mile from the bridge, when we came under heavy phosphorus mortar fire. We all dove for the ditch, which was full of water. We laid there with just our heads out and the mortar shells bursting on the road beside us. We knew that if any of that burning phosphorus were to hit us, it would be almost impossible to remove and would burn right to the bone. The attack only lasted for a few minutes. I guess the Germans thought they had chased us away, or else they ran out of mortar shells.

Very quickly thereafter, the sergeant major came up in his jeep and ordered us to continue across the bridge. We made it over without any further opposition, and took over an empty house that was nearby. We planned to be there for a few days and wanted to establish radio silence. Therefore, we had to get a telephone line across the canal. My partner and I were sent back to pick up the end of the line, which headquarters was going to toss across the canal to us.

The Germans turned their coastal guns around and started firing toward us. We nicknamed the projectiles freight trains, as they were so large that they eventually flipped end over end, causing a chug, chug, chug sound similar to a steam engine. Some of them were quite close. I guess they must have scared off the headquarters crew, as we searched up and down the canal, futilely calling to the crew who were supposed to be throwing the line over to us.

About midnight we gave up and started to return to our company, but we had to locate the place where we would be able to jump across the deep water-filled ditch to the road. We searched up and down for quite some time before finding a place which we thought was the right one. I jumped first, but it turned out to be just some floating bog. I went into the water up to my neck. My partner grabbed my rifle and pulled me out. This was in mid-October, and it was cold! We finally found a place where we were able to jump across and get back to the road.

We knew that we had to go to the right, or we would be heading toward the enemy lines. As it was, we discovered we were about an eighth of a mile behind the enemy lines when we came upon a German dugout near the road, with three or four Germans in there talking. They had their flashlight lit, so we were able to see them, but we were in no position to take them on by ourselves. We had no grenades and my rifle, the only one we had with us, was full of water. Silently, we snuck past and made it back to our company.

We were in a shelled-out building with no roof, just the four walls and a cement floor. Wet and cold, I crawled in between a couple of guys; they told me, "Get the h… out of here, that shiver is catching." So, I moved over to a corner by myself.

13

THEY GOT ME!!

It was the middle of October 1944. About a week or so after crossing over the Leopold Canal, we were in a yard with a high board fence, on the outskirts of town. I peeked between the boards, and saw that the yard next door was full of German soldiers wandering around. We started a skirting attack through a flooded field with water up to our knees.

Soon, we came under heavy machine gun fire. We made it to a road, and regrouped in the ditch on the other side. Lying flat on my stomach, I had the officer's field glasses, and was scanning the area that the machine gun fire had been coming from. I observed two German soldiers coming across a field, carrying a white flag. Our officer ordered us to hold our fire.

As soon as they got close, the Germans dropped down into a shell hole, and as they did, I saw they had bazookas (shoulder-fired anti-tank weapons) on their backs. I advised the officer accordingly. He ordered us to head toward the canal behind us. We hadn't gone far when a bazooka projectile landed a few feet to my right. Thank goodness it landed in soft mud and buried itself somewhat before exploding. Consequently, most of the shrapnel went over my head, but not all of it. I was wounded! I am still carrying shrapnel to this day.

I was in hospital in Belgium for a few days. The first morning in the hospital, the nurse came to me and said she would wash up as far as possible, and down as far as possible, and I could wash "possible". She proceeded to lift the covers off my feet to start with the first part of her task. As soon as she saw my dark black feet, she got the strangest look on her face. I think her first thought was that my feet were rotting off. Immediately upon seeing her reaction, I told her that I had lost my Canadian army boots and was wearing British boots. The dye came out of them when they got wet.

Infection from the shrapnel in my groin had spread to my leg. The leg was swollen so badly that it looked like a stove pipe. They had to lance it at the knee and drain the infection. I was taken by ambulance to Ostend, Belgium, to be transferred to a waiting hospital ship. But when the ambulance arrived at Ostend, there was an air raid in progress, and I had to wait it out in a British army hospital.

A little Polish nurse working there came to give me my shot of penicillin. To my surprise, it was nothing like my previous experience with the gigantic needle and syringe in the Canadian field hospital. She gave me the shot in my arm, rather than the butt, with a small syringe and a very small needle. I thought to myself, "Why couldn't the Canadian nurses do it like that?"

Before long the air raid ended, and the "all clear" was sounded. I was transferred to an ambulance and taken on board the hospital ship, to be transported across the English Channel to a hospital in England.

Eventually I recovered, and after being discharged from hospital near the end of November 1944, I was given some leave and went to London. Arriving at Waterloo Station, I stood in awe at its enormous size, and suddenly felt lost. This was my first leave in England, and I was all alone. I got myself a scone and coffee at an armed forces snack bar (NAAFI) and stood there wondering where I should go.

A Canadian air force chap approached me and asked me where I was staying. I replied that I had no idea, and that I had just arrived. He suggested that I go with him to the Canadian Legion Club on Gower Street, where he was staying, and so I did.

Navy, Army, Air Force Institution

Inside N.A.A.F.I

Mother and Uncle of my Aunt Florence

My Aunt Florence in Dartmouth, Nova Scotia, had given me her mother's address, so I decided to take a couple of days and visit her. She lived at Gravesend across the Thames River from the Tilbury Docks, just outside London. Aunt Florence's mother had a small three-story apartment. She and her young niece with a baby slept on the second floor. I slept with her brother Bill on the third floor.

A short while after going to bed, the air raid siren sounded. I asked Bill if we should go down to the shelter. He replied, "I figure if my time has come, I might as well die in bed." After living through years of air raid sirens screaming and bombs exploding, a lot of people must have become tired of running every time a siren sounded.

We wouldn't have had time to go to a shelter anyway, as suddenly there was a terrific boom and the building shook. But it wasn't long before the 'all clear' sounded, and we went to sleep.

The next morning my hostess fried me up a plate of fish eggs. I don't like fish, and I certainly don't care for fish eggs. Since food was rationed, however, and I didn't have any ration coupons, I realized that this dear woman was making the most of whatever was available. I certainly tried not to let her see that I was having difficulty swallowing; in fact I was nearly choking on every mouthful. When she offered to cook up another plateful for me, I had an awful time convincing her that I was full!

After breakfast we walked down the street a couple of blocks, where a V-2 rocket bomb had hit. It had destroyed a large part of a city block, leaving a huge crater. I don't think being in a shelter would have saved the people where this bomb hit.

V-2 Rocket Bomb

The V-2 was an early German ballistic missile, first introduced in September of 1944. It was mostly used against British and Belgian targets, to terrorize and demoralize the population. Programmed to hit a particular target, the V-2 was more accurate than the buzz bomb. Carrying over 2,000 pounds (more than a ton) of explosives, its overall weight was nearly 12 tons. It travelled at 3,550 kilometers per hour, powered by a liquid oxygen/alcohol mixture. Launched from mobile launching pads in France, its range was approximately 100 to 110 km. From launch to impact was about 3 minutes, which gave very little warning of an attack. It has been estimated that there were 2,754 civilians killed and 6,523 civilians injured by the V-2 rocket.

After visiting my aunt's family, I returned to the Canadian Legion Club for the remainder of my leave, which I spent with the air force chap. We toured the Tower of London, St. Paul's Cathedral, the Parliament Buildings, Westminster Abbey, the Old Bailey Law Court, and many other attractions. We got quite efficient at using The Underground, as they called the subway. While we were at the Old Bailey, we watched a murder trial which was in progress, and we found that very interesting.

One evening we went to meet the parents of my air force pal's girlfriend in Southall, outside London. We missed the last train back to London that night. If we were to wait at the station, we could take the milk train. This was the last train until morning, delivering the milk to London, and carrying the workers returning home from their shift.

Upon our arrival in London, between one and two o'clock in the morning, there was an air raid in progress, and all the lights were out. The buses and The Underground were shut down, so we had to walk from Paddington Station to Gower Street, about six miles in the dark. We had a map of London that we were trying to follow, because we didn't know our way on surface. At every intersection there was a little post about four feet tall with a dim light inside. The light shone straight out, not up or down, so enemy aircraft couldn't see it. We would hold the map very close to the slot in order to read it, and thus were able to keep checking our directions.

After my leave was over, I was sent to Cove, where I spent Christmas and New Year's.

14

YA GOTTA BE TOUGH!

In January of 1945, a number of new officers arrived at Cove from Canada. Some of the troops that had seen action, including myself, were given the task of taking these officers on a week's scheme, to give them an idea of how we did things at the front. We had a truck in which we carried the cooking equipment and other equipment that was needed on the scheme. All our meals were cooked outside, and we slept in the snow banks. We each had a rubberized canvas ground sheet and one thick wool army blanket. To make our bed, we spread the ground sheet on the snow, folded our blanket in half lengthwise, and if we removed our tunic, we used it for a pillow. Then we would put our wool greatcoat over top.

One evening I came across a place where there was a five foot steel culvert. I thought this was an ideal place for my bed, but it turned out to be the worst possible place. The steel culvert was just sucking every ounce of heat from my body, and I had to get up in the middle of the night and move my bed out into a snow bank.

Another night I made my bed down under a little clump of bushes. The cook used to make us a cup of coffee or hot chocolate, and would give us a biscuit to go with it before we went to bed. The spot where I had made my bed down was across a little creek. On the way over to get my hot chocolate, I broke through the ice into water above my knees. After having my hot chocolate, I went back over the creek to my bed, took off my tunic for a pillow, and removed my wet trousers, putting them between my blanket and greatcoat. I put my boots on either side of me under my greatcoat, and went to sleep. In the morning when I woke up, I was covered in about three or four inches of light snow. My boots and trousers had dried out and I got dressed. I never even caught a sniffle.

I returned to Antwerp, Belgium in February, 1945. I took the train to Ghent, where I was stationed in a holding unit. There I waited to be recalled to the Royal Winnipeg Rifles, if and when they needed a replacement signaler. The first while, I was stationed at St. Peter's Barracks. There were bunks, but no mattresses and no blankets. The glass in most of the windows was broken. All we had was our ground sheet and one blanket. There was a fireplace, but we were very short of wood, and the fire wasn't kept going at night. During the day, we would roast on one side and freeze on the other. Some of the guys were so cold that they resorted to breaking up and burning some of the empty bunks.

The 'toilet' was the type that could be hosed down at the same time as they hosed down the floor. There were no doors on the stalls for privacy. There wasn't even a seat to sit on. It was simply a sunken drain in the floor, with two cement pads to stand on and bars on each side to hang onto, while you hung your bottom out to do your duty.

'Toilet' at St. Peter's Barracks

Eventually we were transferred to Leopold Barracks, where I remained until shortly after Victory in Europe (V.E.) Day. There we had very little heat in the building, and we slept on a cold marble floor, again with only a ground sheet and one blanket. When we went to bed, it felt like a marble floor; when we woke up in the morning, it might as well have been a feather bed, as we were so numb we couldn't feel anything.

While there I came down with ulcerative stomatitis and had to go to the hospital, because I needed to be on a liquid diet. I don't think you could have put the point of a toothpick anywhere inside my mouth without touching an ulcer. It brought tears to my eyes just to swallow. Otherwise I was fine.

One day I asked the nurse if I could watch an operation while I was there. She replied, "I don't know, but I'll check on it." Later she informed me that if I went to the operating room at eight o'clock in the morning, I could watch some.

During the first one, the doctor lanced the chap's knee, which wasn't very exciting. The next operation was an appendectomy. I stood at the chap's right shoulder. The orderly was at his left shoulder, the nurse to the left side, and the doctor to his right. When he got so far as the hard layer surrounding the abdomen, I thought maybe that was the bowel, and was concerned that the doctor might cut it by mistake. I wasn't looking forward to that happening, so I guess I went a little white. The doctor must have been keeping an eye on me, as he suggested that the orderly had better take me out for some fresh air. I told him I was okay, and he instructed the orderly to keep an eye on me.

When the operation was over, the doctor told me that I had done better than most interns, as they usually flaked out on the first operation they watched. I was surprised when I saw that the patient lost less than a teaspoon of blood during the whole surgery. I think now that it was very good for me to have seen this, as before then I had always dreaded the thought of ever having an operation. The nurse that I had spoken to previously insisted that I should go through to be a doctor.

While I was in the hospital, the Red Cross worker offered to give me crochet, knitting, or embroidery work to keep myself occupied. I chose the latter, and embroidered a place mat, which she told me included every stitch used in embroidery. I sent it to my mother, who framed it in a tray.

I did various jobs that were assigned to me, one being guarding a Canadian soldier who had been caught after being absent without leave. He wasn't worried about how he behaved, as he expected to be given a dishonorable discharge. While being AWOL, he had stolen an American officer's uniform and an American tanker truck. He would go to the American compound every night, where they stored the gasoline, and fill the tanker. Then he would sell the fuel on the French black market during the day. He said that he had made enough money

My Embroidery

on the black market in Paris that he had bought a hotel there, and his girlfriend was running it for him. He was just waiting for his court-martial and discharge, and he figured he would have it made. I have no idea how he made out.

Awhile before VE Day, May 8, 1945, I was asked if I would like to be a batman for Dr. Kohn, a Canadian doctor at St. Peter's Barracks in Ghent. The job required that I make his bed, press his uniform, and polish his boots. (My own uniform and boots never looked so good!) I was also free to go downtown whenever I had spare time. They advised me that I would have heated quarters and a cot to sleep on. It sure sounded good to me. So that's what I did until VE Day, at which time Dr. Kohn returned to Canada.

15

ARMY OF OCCUPATION

Qualification to return to Canada was on a point system. As I had only been overseas for a short while before D-Day, I did not have enough points to come back to Canada at that time. Had I been called back as replacement with the Royal Winnipeg Rifles, the point system would not have come into play, as I would have returned to Canada with the regiment. Consequently, I was required to stay on as part of the Army of Occupation for a further length of time.

Lake Superior Regiment Hat Badge

A stamped brass and silver alloy badge measuring approximately 5.5cm x 4.5cm. It consists of a central silver alloy disc with "The Lake Superior Regiment" to the perimeter, with a stylized "LSR" to the center. A wreath of maple leafs that is intersected at the top by the profile of a beaver and a scroll with the motto "Inter Pericula Intrepidi" or "Fearless Amid Danger".

I was transferred to the Lake Superior Regiment as part of the Army of Occupation. We moved to Zoost, Holland, for a short while, and then to Hengelo, near the German border.

The signalers were always positioned alongside the officers spearheading the attacks. We carried our two-way radio on our backs. We had to be close enough to the officer that he could take the mike and talk into it from time to time. Sometimes he would just give us the message that he wanted sent. Whenever the regiment was static, we would still be busy laying telephone line, operating the telephone exchange, and manning the telephone in the orderly rooms at night.

The regimental sergeant major had been an infantry signaler previous to working his way up through the ranks. On parade the first morning, the sergeant major announced that everyone had to attend parade daily, except the signalers, as they had earned a rest. The only parades we were told to attend were meal parade and pay parade, and even those were optional.

It wasn't quite that way, because I was attached to a company, and the signalers in the company were required to go to regimental headquarters, where we would take shifts operating the telephone exchange one week per month. The

Operating the Telephone Exchange at LSR Headquarters

other three weeks, we took turns sleeping at the company orderly room to answer the phone.

In our company the signalers set up a dark room, developing films and printing pictures for members of the regiment who wanted this done. This turned out to take a lot of our time. We charged the fellows so many cigarettes to develop a film and print their pictures.

The Lake Superior Regiment decided to go back to Normandy and retrace their steps from there to Holland. We took a side trip from this to visit the Vimy Memorial of the First World War. That was certainly worth seeing. When we arrived back in Holland, some fellows who had acquired really good German cameras had taken many rolls of film, which they now brought to us to develop and print for them. Often they didn't know how to operate the cameras properly, so most of the films had less than 10% of the pictures worth printing. The Padre had an old Eastman Kodak box camera that he had brought overseas with him. Close to 100% of his pictures were nearly perfect. We ended up making copies of his pictures for anyone in the regiment who wanted a set. This kept us really busy!

Cigarettes were used as currency. We even used them at the store to buy our supplies for the dark room. There was a shortage of cigarettes, and Canadian cigarettes especially were more valuable than the currency itself, so we would get better value for cigarettes in trade.

We signalers made our own photo enlarger
using a plate camera.

To My Dear Mother

One of the chaps in the regiment was a sketch artist. He would charge a certain number of cigarettes for each sketch. He made a sketch of their choice for each member of the regiment, and then bartered for cigarettes. I am including a copy of the sketch I purchased for my mother.

16

OOOH LA LA!

Another chap and I from the Lake Superior Regiment had our names drawn for a ten day leave in Paris. There were two soldiers' names randomly drawn from each regiment for this vacation. I would imagine it was an ongoing thing, and a way to rejuvenate the troops and break the boredom.

We stayed at the Grande Hŏtel, which was the hotel that our King and Queen used to stay at whenever they were in Paris before the war. The two of us shared a room. We would leave our uniforms and boots by the door overnight, and they would be pressed and polished for us in the morning. We ate our meals in the same beautiful dining room with high-arched ceilings showing incredible painted scenes. We got the same service as anyone staying there before the war. The silverware extended on both sides of the plate for about six inches. All the waiters were dressed in tuxedos, and the menus, I'm sure, were the same as before the war. We could choose anything we wanted off the menu.

Every evening they brought in three bus loads of young ladies to a ball held in the huge ballroom. I didn't dance, but I enjoyed watching. I got talking to one of the military police, whose job was to ensure that none of the ladies would leave the ballroom at any time during the evening. If any of them did so, they would not be invited back for any other evening.

He asked me if I would like to go for a ride on his motorcycle after the ball was over, as he had to escort one of the bus loads of ladies to their homes in many locations in Paris. I accepted!

It was a beautiful, warm evening in May. After seeing that they all arrived home safely, he brought me back to the hotel. This was a wonderful holiday. Everything at the hotel: the room, the meals, the ball, was paid for by the army.

Eiffel Tower, First Level

We toured the Arc de Triomphe with the Tomb of the Unknown Soldier, The Mint, the Palais de Concord, Napoleon's Tomb directly beneath the Dome Church at the Hŏtel des Invalides, and the Madeleine Church. The latter lies directly between two busy street, and has no windows, only three skylights. We rode The Metro (metropolitan subway) to many other places and became quite the experts. Their system was very easy to understand.

Sacré Coeur (Church of the Sacred Heart)

We took a bus tour to Sacré Coeur, the Church of the Sacred Heart, where we had to climb the 'Stairs of A Hundred Steps' leading up to the church. It was a very beautiful church, but the one thing that stuck out in my mind was the two large pillars out in front with the maps of Paris. The map on the top of each pillar had a picture of each of the important sites inserted onto it. There was a line drawn from each picture back to the edge where you would stand. You could look at the picture, line up the line from you to the picture, and see that particular building in the distance beyond the end of that line.

Notre Dame Cathedral

Another highlight of our holiday in Paris was the tour of
Notre Dame Cathedral. One of the most outstanding features
of the cathedral was the carvings in the three archways in
front of the main doors. These carvings were of every biblical
figure. I can see why it's known as one of the most beautiful
cathedrals in Europe. I really enjoyed that holiday. It is one
good wartime memory that I was able to take home.

17

HOLLAND:
MY HOME FOR A TIME

After returning to the regiment in Hengelo, Holland, I managed to get permission to go to the artillery company which was stationed nearby, to see my cousin Norris Pringle. I spent a couple of days with him there just before they returned to England on their way back to Canada.

A lot of the Canadian troops acquired German guns and ammunition of one sort or another, with the intention of bringing them home for souvenirs. The order was posted that anyone caught with firearms or ammunition of any type during an inspection that would be done, would remain in the Army of Occupation rather than going back home. A large, deep pit was dug, and everyone with any of these items was supposed to throw them into the pit as they marched past. Then fuel was dumped into the hole, and everything was set on fire. It was a noisy place for awhile!

The first while that we were in Hengelo, four other fellows in the regiment and myself were billeted with Everett and Jenny VanVe. I slept by myself in a small room with a single bed on the third floor. We were only there for a short while, when the regiment found quarters for us on the other side of the city, which was closer to the camp.

While we were there, and since it was the fall of the year, we asked them whether they had ever eaten corn on the cob.

They replied in dismay, "Oh, corn is only for the animals!"

We told them that we eat it in Canada. In the fall of the year it is something that we all look forward to, a good feed of corn on the cob! Then we asked them whether they would prepare it for us, if we were to get some. Jenny said she would.

We went to the market, where we were able to buy some cobs of field corn, and we got some butter from our cook. We showed Jenny how to boil it in some salted water, and then coat it with butter and eat it right off the cob.

They said they didn't know that it was so delicious! In all the years when food was so short during the German occupation, they had fed the corn to the animals. We told her that we have a different variety of corn in Canada. As well as the field corn, we also have table corn that we grow only for ourselves. We ate all of the corn that we had picked up, and I'm sure that Jenny and Everett probably would have continued to eat corn after we left.

Everett and Jenny VanVe, in Hengelo, Holland

Dutch Children in their Traditional Dress

18

BACK TO ENGLAND

The Lake Superior Regiment moved back to England before Christmas, 1945, on their way home. We were transported across the English Channel on a merchant marine ship.

Once again we were packed in like sardines with all our equipment. The quarters were stuffy and I couldn't sleep. I went up on deck and lay down on the port side against a wall, where I slept all night. The channel was quite rough, with a north east wind blowing. It was a good job that the channel didn't get any rougher, as I likely would have ended up overboard. There were just cables between me and the water, and as the boat rocked, I could easily have rolled beneath the cables and landed in the drink.

We went to a military camp in England, where we were trained on parade everyday by the senior regimental sergeant major of the British permanent forces. He was preparing our Lake Superior Regiment to receive the King's Colors, which were going to be presented by King George VI after New Year's. After pounding the parade square from morning to night for many days, the day finally came for our regiment to receive the King's Colors.

It was a cool, drizzly morning when we were called on parade. We stood there for almost an hour waiting for the King to come. Two of the soldiers passed out. We were eventually broken off, and told to go and change into dry uniforms, after which we returned on parade and waited in the rain once more.

Eventually a number of cars arrived. Our commanding officer was advised that the King was ill, and that Viscount Alexander had come to present the colors in his place. The Viscount almost ran up and down the ranks during the inspection, while having someone hold an umbrella over his head. He presented the colors very rapidly, quickly returned to his vehicle, and they all drove off.

I'm certain that if the King had been well, this ceremony would have been more formal, and much more meaningful. Viscount Alexander sure didn't leave a very good impression with the troops. On top of the way the presentation was handled, the troops were really put out, to put it mildly, to think that our own sergeant major, having put his life on the line for the British in action, wasn't good enough to train the regiment to receive the King's colors.

While in England, a friend of mine had received permission to marry his English girlfriend in Brighton. As I was to be his best man, Mike arranged leave for me to go to the wedding. We were in England for Christmas, and as Mike was still on leave, I managed to spend a couple of days with him and his new wife. On Christmas Eve, they invited me out to dinner. Later in the evening they went home, and that was the last time I saw them. I don't recall what arrangements he had made regarding his return to Canada, or whether he did return.

On my way back to the hostel, I was walking down Marine Drive, which was the street overlooking the English Channel, lined with expensive hotels. During the tourist season it would have been very busy, but that night there was almost no one in sight.

Finally, I came upon a couple of British air force chaps and two British air force women. They had dropped a book, which had come apart on the sidewalk, and they were trying to gather it up. They appeared to be a little inebriated, so I stopped and gathered up the book, handing it to them. They said, "O Canada, come and have a drink with us!"

I declined, but they kept insisting that I join them for a drink. I was wearing the Lake Superior Regiment badge and flashes, and have been told that the 'Lake Sups' had been billeted in Brighten before D-Day. So I thought that maybe these were people who had known some of them, and maybe they just wanted to express their appreciation. I finally agreed to go and have a drink with them.

We hadn't gone very far before they turned into the gate of one of the luxury hotels. Instead of going to the main door, they all went down a flight of stairs to the basement level. They rang the bell and someone came to let us in. We walked down a long hallway, and finally came to a doorway, where we entered a room filled with people ranging from perhaps twenty to seventy years of age.

Upon entering I was given a beer. I sat down on a chair along the wall near the doorway that I had just come through. For some time I was just ignored and I began to feel very much out of place. I wished I had never accepted their offer. Eventually, one of the air force chaps came over and knelt down in front of me. He said, "What will you have, Canada? You can have any one of us, or any one of the women!"

I immediately thought, "Whoa, I've heard of where guys have been in this type of situation and ended up in the gutter the next morning with their wallets gone!" I was also somewhat embarrassed, because of the elderly people in the room, and wasn't about to make any kind of a fuss. But though I steadily refused his offer, he just kept begging me to take him up on it.

All the time I was getting more nervous and more embarrassed, when all of a sudden one of the air force women came along and said to him, "Not yet, Jock, wait awhile."

"Boy", I thought, "You are all tarred with the same stick." I didn't know what to do. I knew that the door was locked, and even if it wasn't, I had to get down that long hallway. I sat there and kept telling him that I wasn't interested in either of them, but he wasn't about to give up.

Suddenly the door bell rang. One of the ladies in the room left to go to the door and I thought, "Now's my chance!"

Quickly I said to Jock, "I want to drink a toast to you!" He first had to get on his feet and pick up his beer from the table behind him. I dropped my beer and took off like a jack rabbit, out that door and down the hall, almost knocking over the people at the front door. I never stopped running until I was a couple of blocks down the street. I'll bet I was the most frightened 22 year-old in Brighton that night.

19

HOMEWARD BOUND

SS Ile de France

I headed to Canada in early February 1946, aboard the *SS Ile de France*. Again I was on D-deck, this time on the starboard side. There was a really bad winter storm on the go in the North Atlantic. Now I got a chance to appreciate the advice that Billy Pringle had given me about the dry bread and salt. I was one of the fortunate few onboard who were not horribly seasick.

At the stern of the ship there was a huge spiral staircase. When the ship was rising up over a wave, it was a gigantic effort to take one step up the stairs. Then, as you were straining to take the next step, the ship would slide over the crest and down the other side, and you would suddenly fly up about five or six steps all at once. After two or three times doing this, a lot of the troops headed for the railing at the center of the stairs, hung their heads over, and threw up.

The trip back was otherwise uneventful, except one night the crew told us they had hit a rogue wave about eighty feet high, and it had torn a gun turret off the bow of the ship. That trip was definitely not as enjoyable as the earlier trip going overseas had been!

After arriving at Halifax, we boarded a train headed west across Canada to drop off troops at different points. We travelled first class all the way! That was a big difference from our trip eastward, when we had been heading for overseas. That time, we were in sleeper cars, but the beds had no mattresses. We didn't have the usual dining car, but rather a freight car with long tables and benches, where they served us our meals.

On the way home, we made a stop at one Maritime station, where a ladies' auxiliary boarded the train and gave each of our troops an *Oh Henry* chocolate bar. At another stop the ladies' auxiliary gave each of us a banana. Those were appreciated by all, as we didn't get either overseas!

Later on, as we were traveling around a huge hill, the smaller wheels on the front of the second engine came off the rails. The second engineer applied the brakes to stop the train. The first engineer opened his throttle wide open, and was able to hold the second engine on the rails. Had he not managed to do so, the train could have ended up in the valley 1000 feet or so below. We had to wait while the wheels were jacked back onto the rails, then we travelled slowly until we were able to change the engine.

At Port Arthur we got off the train and were led by the ladies' pipe band, as we were marched to Fort William armory about a half mile away. There they had a wonderful meal ready for us. Meanwhile, the train moved up to Fort William, where we boarded again. Upon reaching our individual destinations, the troops all began two weeks of furlough.

As I got off the train and headed into the station, my mother and youngest sister Doreen were waiting for me. As soon as Doreen saw me, she ran toward me and threw her arms around my neck. She had grown and changed so much in the two years I had been overseas that I didn't recognize her, and pushed her to one side. Of course it broke her heart, and she began to cry. I had thought she was just a beautiful young girl that was meeting the troops to show her appreciation to them. When I reached my mother, she told me that the girl was Doreen! Of course I apologized to my sister, explaining that she had grown to be such a beautiful young lady that I hadn't recognized her. She felt much better then.

My mother, Doreen, and I spent a couple of days in Winnipeg, shopping and visiting with relatives. After returning to Darlingford, I developed a boil on my nose beside my left eye, and I had to go to the hospital in Morden, where they lanced it. Again, I was given the daily penicillin shot in the butt. A young ward aid used to laugh her head off every time she saw me getting this 'abusive' treatment.

One day the nurse came in to give me my shot, and I said to her, "You aren't giving me the shot today!"

She inquired, "Why? Is there something wrong with the way I give it to you?"

I said, "No, there isn't, but Polly is giving me the shot today."

She replied, "Oh, she can't give it; she's only a ward aid!"

I said, "If I say so, I guess she can, can't she?"

She answered, "If you say so, I guess she can," and she called the aid over. She told Polly, "You're giving him the shot today."

I couldn't see, because they were behind me, but I gather that she showed Polly how to do it. After that, when the nurse came in to give me the shot, Polly would be long gone!

Later, when I lived in Flin Flon, I got to know Polly's sister and brother-in-law. When Polly came up to visit, they invited my brother and me down for dinner one evening, and we had a good laugh over telling the story again.

When I returned home from the hospital, I enjoyed the remainder of my furlough visiting with my mother, my twin sister Edna, and other relatives and friends.

One morning I was visiting Edna at her house. There had been a fairly heavy snowfall during the night. Upon hearing a train approaching, her young daughter rushed to the window. Edna asked Barbara, "Is there anything in front of the engine?" Edna was thinking there might be a snowplow in front.

Barbara's response was, "The tracks, of course!"

After my furlough ended, I returned to No. 10 District Depot in Winnipeg. While waiting for my discharge, a bunch of us were on the depot steps, when the regimental sergeant major of the permanent force rode by in an open jeep.

Without thinking I hollered, "Hey, your wheels are turning!" The words just popped out of my mouth. Immediately he had the driver back up the jeep and stop. From his vehicle he demanded to know who it was that had shouted. We were all veterans, and none of them squealed on me. Finally he gave up and drove away. I don't know what the outcome might have been if one of the fellows had squealed!

Discharged from the armed forces on March 14, 1946 at twenty-two years of age, I received a return ticket from the army to Flin Flon, Manitoba. My Uncle Harvey, who lived there, had told me there was plenty of work available. The return part of the ticket I never did use. I spent the next 40 years in that community, where I met my wife and raised a family of four.

20

I'M A CIVILIAN AGAIN

Upon first moving to Flin Flon, I stayed with my aunt and uncle for a little while, as I searched for employment. I hired on with the Hudson Bay Mining and Smelting Company, Ltd. Though I had tried to get onto the electrical crew, I was unable due to the fact that the electricians' seniority had carried on during the time that they were in the armed forces. As they returned, they were now bumping the electricians off that had been hired during the war. So I ended up working for eight months on the bull gang in the zinc plant tank house.

I wanted to go home to Darlingford for Christmas, but holidays were allotted on a seniority basis. Now, I had also been working part time for Sutton Pettersen Ltd., doing their radio and appliance repairs. So I suggested to them that I quit the company, go home for Christmas, and work for them full time when I got back. Sutton Pettersen actually agreed to this and hired me on full-time. I worked for them for ten years, and eventually became manager.

While I was working for Sutton Pettersen, the restaurant across the street had just been taken over by Clinton Reynolds, and his cooks were having trouble with the oven. Clint came over and asked me if I would go and check out the oven. I did, and found there was nothing wrong.

The next day Clint came over 'madder than a hatter'! He told me that the oven was still burning the cakes, which weren't rising at all. He was serving them as sponge cake with vanilla sauce over the top! So I advised him that I would go back and recheck the oven.

Again, I found the oven to be operating perfectly, but his cooks claimed that it definitely was not! So I told Clint to have the cooks whip up a cake ready to put into the oven at eight o'clock that evening, and I would come over and bake it, myself. He agreed to take me up on the challenge.

Now, I had never baked a cake before in my life. So I went back to the store, and I got a manual from one of the new ranges on the floor, and started studying it. When the store closed at six o'clock, I hurried to my Aunt Lila's house, and asked her to tell me how to bake a cake. I told her the whole story. Although she didn't have an electric range, she advised me that you *must* pre-heat the oven to the correct temperature before you put the cake in. She also told me *not* to open the door of the oven until about two minutes before the cake was due to be finished baking. Otherwise, the colder air would cause the cake to fall. She also showed me how high to fill the cake pan with the batter, and told me the correct temperature to bake it at. Armed with this information, I headed for the restaurant at eight o'clock, as agreed upon earlier.

The cook had just finished mixing up the cake batter. She poured it into the cake pan, and I quickly noticed that the pan was almost completely filled with the batter. I advised her that it was way too much. She insisted that it had to be that full, because otherwise the cake wouldn't rise high enough. I told her to get another pan and take about half the batter out. She was reluctant to do this, but I insisted, telling her that *I* was baking the cake, and she needed to follow my instructions. So she brought a couple of muffin tins, and spooned the excess batter into them. Then she wanted to put a second pan beneath the cake to keep it from burning on the bottom. I objected strongly, and she took it away.

In the meantime, I had told her that we had to preheat the oven, which she argued with me about. Once again, I insisted that *I* was the one doing the baking!

By this time the oven was preheated, so I put the cake in and checked the time. About half way through, the cook wanted to open the oven, as she was certain the cake would be burning. I managed to intercept her in time. When the prescribed baking time was up, I opened the oven, and there was a beautiful golden brown cake, which had nicely risen above the edge of the cake pan.

Then I baked the two muffin tins of batter. When I later opened the oven door, I found that both tins had risen so high, the batter had flowed together, and each tin appeared like a cake!

By this time, Clint had come in. When he saw the cake, he told the cook to put it up on the shelf, and not to serve it until the other cook had come in and seen it. He also warned that the first cook to have a failure after this would be promptly fired! I had definitely won my argument with the cooks about preheating the oven before baking a cake!

Soon I was successful in receiving my Journeyman's and Contractor's Licenses for both Manitoba and Saskatchewan. Also, I obtained my Industrial Electrical Certificate of Qualification with the Interprovincial Seal. During 1947, I started a business of my own, Bert's Record Bar, which I hired a girl to operate. It was a very good winter business, but slowed down considerably during the summer months. Years later, after hiring back on with the H.B.M. & S., I ended up selling the Record Bar to Thompson Electric.

During that time I met Gwen Lund, who was working as a stenographer at the Town Hall office. She also worked as a relief court stenographer and as a relief secretary for various law firms in town. I finally worked up the nerve to ask her for a date, and I was thrilled when she accepted. We were married on July 2, l951. She was then terminated from the Town Hall, as they did not employ married women. Gwen was my Svenska flicka (Swedish girl), the love of my life. She gave me a terrific family of three girls and finally my son, all of whom I am very proud.

Our Wedding

The main highlight of our family's time in Flin Flon was our cabin on Whitefish Lake, about fifteen minutes from town. While I was still a bachelor, my friend Merv Stein and I started to build the cabin from rough logs. It measured twenty-four feet by twenty-six feet.

Merv had the trees all fallen during the winter. In the spring, we went out and peeled off the bark and piled the logs. After the snow was gone, and the weather had warmed sufficiently, Merv and I would go out every weekend, packing cement and spikes a quarter of a mile in from the highway on our backs. We built the foundation pillars from concrete and stone, and then we began raising the log structure. We had the floor down and the walls three logs high, with the framework set for the big living room window and the doors, when my friend and his wife moved to Alberta. My brother Jack and I finished building the log cabin together from that point.

After I was married, I eventually bought the cabin from my brother. I finished chinking the spaces between the logs with a home-made cement mixture consisting of sand, flour, and very hot water. This was very durable, and adhered to the logs better than ordinary cement.

There we spent most of our weekends in the spring and fall of the year, and we would move out to the lake for the entire summer holiday after school was out in June. My kids still rave about their holidays spent boating, fishing, swimming, water-skiing, and exploring.

Our Children (1963)

As the family grew, I built on two extra bedrooms. Ultimately, we talked about retiring at the cabin. That's when I built on a new insulated kitchen, with elaborate new cupboards, a new electric range and refrigerator, and a washroom with flush toilet and shower. It was also plumbed and wired for a washer and dryer. It was the grandchildren who ended up benefitting from the inside toilet!

Our Cabin (1985)

While the children were young, they had a playhouse to keep them busy. When they got older, some of them suggested that they wanted to sleep in a tent with their friends from town. My wife Gwen wasn't comfortable with the idea, because of the bears that sometimes wandered through the property. So I built them a bunkhouse in the bush behind the cabin, complete with electric lights and an intercom to the main cabin. With two sets of bunks, it slept four, and even had the luxury of carpet. We built a second outdoor fireplace nearby for their wiener roasts.

One morning Gwen was busy with company at the cabin. My son Gordon was still sleeping by himself in the bunkhouse out back. Gwen looked through the back cabin window, and saw a black bear sitting on the doorstep of the bunkhouse. She called Gordon on the intercom, and he answered sleepily.

She said, "Gordon, don't come out the door. There's a bear sitting on your doorstep!"

He answered, "Yeah, Mom," and hung up. A few minutes later, she called to warn him again. And once again he responded, "Yeah, Mom," and hung up, sounding even more annoyed.

A while later Gordon came into the cabin. That's when he heard the company talking with my wife about the bear. In disbelief he said, "You mean there really was a bear there? I thought you were fooling!"

The Gazebo (1985)

One of Gwen's favorite places on a hot sunny day was the fifteen foot octagon gazebo I built on concrete pillars, which I sank deeply into the sand. It was screened and carpeted, with full electrical service to cook meals and entertain our friends. My daughters visited years later, and the fellow who had bought the cabin from us told them about having a family graduation party there. He said the old gazebo was completely filled with young people, celebrating and dancing long into the night. He was just waiting for the thing to collapse, and remarked to my girls, "I guess Bert built it right!"

One day in the spring of the year, my wife was out at the cabin putting her bedding plants in the flowerbeds. Being all by herself, she would stand up and look around from time to time, always aware of her surroundings. At one point, she noticed a big cinnamon bear loping up the driveway towards her. Her first thought was to head into the cabin, but to do so would require her to move closer to the bear. She decided that no bear was going to dictate to her where she could go! She grabbed the metal pan beside her, and began banging on it and hollering. The bear turned and quickly headed back down the driveway and out of sight.

Knowing that bears are curious, she continued to keep her eyes open. Sure enough! It had decided to head back and investigate. She grabbed the pan again, and repeated her banging and yelling. The bear turned and left for good this time, and Gwen got all her bedding plants safely in the ground.

In 1956, I was successful in getting onto the electrical crew of the H.B.M. & S. I worked at thirteen different mines that the company operated, all in the Flin Flon area, except one. That one was in the Snow Lake area, and I had to fly in to it.

In 1971, I was promoted to Swing Electrical Foreman, and within a couple of years I became foreman in charge of electrical construction in most of the new mines that were built. Somewhere around 1984, I became Electrical Mine

Foreman of North Main and South Main mines, and Swing Mines Electrical Foreman for all of the Flin Flon mines.

I retired in 1986, after thirty years of service with the HBM&S. Gwen's dream was to live in the sunny Okanagan, to get away from the bitterly cold forty-degree-below winter weather in northern Manitoba. That same year we moved to Vernon, British Columbia, where we enjoyed twenty-two years. After fifty-seven wonderful years of marriage, my wife passed away. I will always miss her.

Since then, I have moved to Portage la Prairie, Manitoba, to be closer to my family.

CONCLUSION

My second-eldest daughter recently asked me, "Dad, how do you feel about war after having been through one?"

My reply was this: "I feel that if all the leaders of the countries were the ones to go to the front lines and fight their own battles, there wouldn't be so many wars!"

All laughing aside, I do recognize that the odd war is required, as when a country is being invaded. Those people then have the right to defend themselves and to receive help in doing so. But I do not believe in these wars where we go into a country and try to change their entire system of government to what we think it should be!

It seems to me that so many don't really understand the underlying cause of World War II. Hitler and his Third Reich may never have come to power, had the general population of Germany not been so poor that they often didn't know where their next meal was coming from. Hitler's plan to build factories to produce his massive war machine, along with the construction of the Audubon highway for its mobilization, ultimately reduced the mass unemployment and provided everyone with a better life. Without forethought as to where this was taking them, the desperate people of Germany blindly went along with their leader's objectives for control, until it was too late.

I sincerely hope history isn't about to repeat itself. When the cost of living continues to rise, more and more of the middle class approach the poverty level, promoting discontent. The number of these people in the line-ups at food banks today is increasing steadily. Being employed is not enough; earning a proper living is what is needed.

When I was a young lad, there were five old retired bachelors living in our area. Each of them received five dollars in social assistance per month, and I'm certain they would likely have starved, had it not been for my dad and others in the area bringing them food regularly. My desire to see the less fortunate being better cared for has continued since that day.

More than fifty countries took part in WWII, and the total cost of the war is said to have been $1,150,000,000,000. Of the 249,500 Canadians who served in World War II, we lost 46,998 men and women, and another 55,000 were wounded.

LEST WE FORGET

A WW II Canadian Cemetery in Europe

ABOUT THE AUTHOR:

Albert Stevens was born on the farm near Darlingford, Manitoba, in the summer of l923. He and his twin sister were among five siblings growing up in the midst of the dustbowl of the 'Dirty Thirties' and the economic woes of the Great Depression.

When Albert was seventeen, his father passed away, and he was left to manage the family farm. The challenges and disappointments of farming included losing to an early frost what had promised to be a bumper crop of flax. By this time World War II was well underway, and he decided to enlist in the RCAF. When it became clear that his options were limited there, and not relishing the prospect of being a tail gunner, he accepted their offer to be discharged in order to join the army.

After the completion of his required training in the army, Albert sailed overseas on the former luxury liner, the *SS Ile de France.* He served as a regimental signaler with the Royal Winnipeg Rifles in France and Belgium, until being wounded in action after the taking of the Leopold Canal. Following his recovery in England, Albert was transferred to the Army of Occupation in Holland as a signaler with the Lake Superior Regiment. Spending Christmas of l945 in England, he later returned to Canada with the regiment on the *Ile de France* in February l946.

Shortly after reuniting with his family, Albert moved to Flin Flon, Manitoba, in search of employment, where he spent the next forty years. There he met and married Gwen Lund, with whom he raised a family of four. After thirty years of service with the Hudson Bay Mining & Smelting Company, Ltd., he retired as an electrical foreman in 1986.

Later that same year Albert and his wife moved to Vernon, British Columbia, where they enjoyed their golden years of retirement in the sunny Okanagan Valley. They resided there for twenty-two years, until Gwen passed away in 2008. He has since returned to Manitoba to be nearer his family, and now resides in the Portage la Prairie area.

Order Form

To order additional copies of No Feather Beds, please use this order form:

Name: ....

Address: ....

City: ....

Prov/State: ....

Postal/Zip Code: ....

Telephone: ( ) ....

_____ copies @ $20 per copy   _____

PLUS:

Delivery in Canada: $3.00 shipping and handling.   _____

Delivery in USA: $6.00 shipping and handling.   _____

TOTAL: _____

Send order form and full payment to:

"No Feather Beds"
Box 88, RR. 3
Portage la Prairie, Manitoba
R1N 3A3

Allow 4 to 6 weeks for delivery

Order Form

To order additional copies of No Feather Beds, please use this order form:

Name: ....

Address: ....

City: ....

Prov/State: ....

Postal/Zip Code: ....

Telephone: ( ) ....

_____ copies @ $20 per copy   _____

PLUS:

Delivery in Canada: $3.00 shipping and handling.   _____

Delivery in USA: $6.00 shipping and handling.   _____

TOTAL: _____

Send order form and full payment to:

"No Feather Beds"
Box 88, RR. 3
Portage la Prairie, Manitoba
R1N 3A3

Allow 4 to 6 weeks for delivery